THE MOSCOW POETRY FILE

2004-2013

poems by

John Huey

Finishing Line Press
Georgetown, Kentucky

THE MOSCOW POETRY FILE

2004-2013

ACKNOWLEDGMENTS

Several of these poems appear in the *Temptation* anthology published in London
by Lost Tower Publications. Other pieces have appeared in *Leannan, Sein und
Werden*, and *The Lost River Review*.

Publisher: Leah Maines

Editor: Christen Kincaid

Cover Art: Gulbatira Abdigalimova

Author Photo: Gulbatira Abdigalimova

Cover Design: Elizabeth Maines McCleavy

Printed in the USA on acid-free paper.
Order online: www.finishinglinepress.com
              also available on amazon.com

Author inquiries and mail orders:
Finishing Line Press
P. O. Box 1626
Georgetown, Kentucky 40324
U. S. A.

Table of Contents

For Gulbatira Abdigalimova

"Не жалею, не зову, не плачу"

Sleeping While Dreaming of You

How did you get in my bones?
How did you get in my blood?
What made you come to me in the center of that
Frozen waste?
Deep Moscow,
What was the ancient magic word you used?
Is that how I saw beneath your eyes,
Into your skin as
It merged into mine
That first night,
All the nights?

Early Days: The Girls
At The Center Of The City

The Moment Being What You Make It

What a place for self-invention!
Never bored!
A lapse in judgment easily forgotten.

You create, recreate, devise all
manner of subterfuge.
Tell endless stories of times past.
Are driven mad with wonders yet to come.

It's the action, the movement that
grabs you.
As has been well noted and remarked
elsewhere, it's an addiction.

And in the end you behave as any
addict might.
Clawing and rummaging through
your time and theirs.
Grasping a leg up or option or
a divestment of some sort.

Anything to keep you up, running and
moving forward.
Here yet another day before you.
All completed by accident of course.

Suddenly you become run down to
nothing and are blown
away as dust.
Flying fast down the wind that blows
West to East.

The jet stream pushing you over
the mountains to the frozen
wastes and steppe beyond.

Which Highway?

Was it the highway out of town or
the road to the center?
That was a decision taken often but
once held prisoner this place
takes you in a
narcotic trance.

A drug like no other I ever had.
It isn't just the sex that traps
you it's the excitement.
The impossibility of being bored while
railing about the prices, danger, corruption.

Immersed in winter in ice mist and stupefying cold.
Lost in frozen mud and the debris of the spirit.
It's you churned up here.

It's a show like no other and
one I never tired of but
like all good shows
it ends.

Like all forms of overstimulation, it
either kills you or sends you
fleeing into the night and
to home in the end though
you will carry it
always as it
carried you.

Short Coats and High Heels

Early on I remember blowing snow
and the two girls,
so lovely in a hard sort of way,
standing, smoking in the storm.
Fairly oblivious of the biting of
the wind blast,
suddenly though,
shivering and actually quite
desperately cold we found a car
to take us in.

The hot breath steamed the
windows and,
dropped off close by after warming,
we chose to shelter next in the
Cathedral where the one who
should have studied her
Atheism in her "Pioneer" days
was seen kneeling,
then lighting a candle for
her long dead mother
who had extinguished
herself far from grace
years before.

A short walk back to the hotel
later there was a hint of
quiet reflection but not a
word of explanation or of
past tears which was,
I found after all,
Their Way.

Snowy Evening

Outside snow finely descending.
Minus twenty, minus twenty five.
Cold, colder I am waiting in the
street for the car to arrive any
moment with the object of
this evenings desire.

A dream caught here.
Anticipation as important as action.
In retrospect I see that when they
started calling I knew I had
arrived.

A regular on the circuit and
a prime prospect.
No, sometimes I thought more than a client.

It took me many months to
figure the real deal here.

All these years later an
honest and upright denizen
of my own space and time
once again.

I sometimes live the dreamland
and landscape of my first days
there and the delicious
delusion of all being
possible where
nothing was ever
denied.

Night Train

At Leningradskiy my first year
there I got the frozen train
North to ancient Veliky Novgorod.
Crossing the night by flicker and
reflection of station,
The coach dining car light bright
with those most stunning
upright girls.
Their looks playing but
my Russian so bad
and their no English
made it just less than
possible to ride the
express to conclusion.
In any case numb from
weeks in Moscow
running the ring roads and
prospekts like all
mad foreigners do in
their earliest "kid" in
proverbial pursuit
within what has
to be the world's
biggest and best
Candy Store.

Road Stop

Middle of the night in the car from the club.
Up to the hotel, just the driver in front and
a genuine Slavic Amazon with me.

Calm in the back minding what we did.
Taking care of the usual night's business.
Real Militia, not idiot road police,
suddenly flagging us down.

The machine gun sort of rudely poking
through the open rear car window butt
up almost against my nose and
the girl starts screaming at them.

Top voice using some harsh Russian words
it seems for emphasis mostly.
In a real tirade for what looked
like a fairly typical late
nighttime shake down.
But she was having none of it!

Later when I asked her what she had
told them that made them let us go
without paying she said she knew
their boss and that they could suck
their OWN dicks.
Tough Lady!

Third Ring Road 2:45 AM

And all six foot plus of
you is crammed in to
the center back of
that Lada with the
tiny bald tires.

Somehow in the glide on
the ice slick track
slipping to that point
where you remember seeing
just such a car,
Smashed and flipped on a winter
road.
No survivors possible in such
circumstances.

And you are not at all concerned being
crammed between two beautiful girls.
Your 'droog' solo in the front seat.

Headed back to the hotel
for such a night that
precludes even the possibility
of such an inconvenient
alternative as
death.

I can categorically confirm
that you really have not lived
until you have taken that
slippery ride down the precipice
with those midnight girls.

Incredible girls,
Cheek by jowl in a
Lada in February in
The Snow.

Great Novgorod Summer 2005

Anna ran the place and all the mafia
Defying girls in their
Covert struggle for
Independence.
19 going on 40 she was the Novgorod
Whirlwind and the youngest
Law student in town.

Number one girl there and she organized
a day for us the like of which
no foreigners in those obscure
parts had seen I think.

With her most stunning friend in tow,
Long afternoon in private banya followed by
an all night party in her
35 year old lady Law
Professors flat.

Absolutely wild it was with everything
Presented at the top level,
Most gracious of Russian hospitality and
All hands on deck.

At dawn awake alone and caught a
glimpse of her in the other room
with her teacher,
Naughty girls to start the day, as
Was so often the case up there,
With joy.

Later they all came with the broadest
Of smiles to kiss us goodbye on
The street when the car came,
All of us squinting in that
Slanted northern sunlight,
All young (though some old) and

Free and happy in the
Moment once again.

Libertines of the Golden Ring

Lobby sitters working here
not as interesting
or lovely as
the more developed
educated girls in
the better clubs.
There is a female pimp
running the show in
this mostly Russian
joint, she like some
sort of slutty provincial
"Duena" or
dirty Mother Superior,
watching the customers and
counting up the sums,
calculating.
Here it's mostly mobbed up
Slavic types as well as
the usual Center Hotel run
of German, British, French,
Italian global
sales leaders with the
"odd" North American
thrown into the nest.
All sitting here watching the
older "akula" who swim
deliberately,
as all sharks do, while
consulting with a few, fresher,
newly arrived harlots who pass
one from the other
giving shouted advice
on the way out, which, it seems,
translated back,
is something like,
"Watch out for that one."

Strippers

You might BE sleazy but
it's impossible to FEEL
sleazy here.
Girls so fine, well spoken,
elegant and calm.

Amazing in their mental as
well as other, more obvious,
dexterity but definitely
focused on stripping the
client as naked as
they are.

The real music here the
sound of ruble, euro,
dollar, pound, ruble, euro,
dollar, pound.
Cash flying, flying!

The best places like
this the world over.
Run with a level of
professionalism that,
if applied to industry,
could lead to Chinese
market shares and
Japanese quality.

Sadly enough for the beleaguered
public at large, only here do
controls and efficiencies
on this scale apply making
any Vegas or LA joint the
abject failures they
are when compared to
such as these.

If these club owners had
been in charge they
would have beaten us
to the moon.

Miramistin

Health conscious girls and boys,
ordering it by the gallon.
Elixir of life, "Aqua Alta"
of Moscow.

Streets washed in it.
Bathers in excess,
Fountains in front of
the discos.
Splashing in post dance all
souls gathered at the
midnight "aptecka"
to order up more and more.

It is about as essential
for a Saturday night in this
town as Viagra at a
banya.

Receptions are thrown with
punch bowls full and
given as bottled favors
in swag bags at all the
downtown parties.

As necessity meets reality
it was good Post-Soviet
stuff from the space program
designed to wipe germs
from "rockets".

Now wiping down other
things.

After going all night long
there's nothing like it.

I actually saw someone
gargle with it
at 6:00 AM one
morning.

Sex

Sex here makes a philosopher of you.
It evolves from the young man's
ideal made flesh
To concrete reality
To the abstract where
you give study to
what moves
from dark angel
To shark
To life.

Then you are altered by truth and a
strong woman's heart.
Knowing what it might mean
sometime in this existence
to find a visible partner.

Their fantasy was my reality and
literally true beyond description.
What could be considered a dream there?
With subtle impact,
Soft turning in the night with the glow.
How could this fortunate Western son
Have been me?

Altered States

It was at 4:00AM or so one evening in
my early Moscow years.
In a room on Tverskaya that night I saw
it most clearly crystallized
in the eyes of the women
of the center.
All aware that the state we had
achieved in the dark was not only
heightened but "spiritual" in a
way I had heard believers
describe their relations.
True Evensong.

Them, dreaming of an outer world ruled
by the invisible.
Us, our belief rooted in the tangible.

At home, across the waters, in
A bleak and uncomprehending place,
We would be discounted and reviled
As trivial, wrapped in worldly
Trappings, steeped in sin.

Those Pilgrims could have only a dream of being
Wrapped in the truthful transports of flesh and
Spirit.

Here, imbued with not a small measure of intellect,
All is well that takes you to the light.
All is bright that settles in you with both
Reason and a far superior
State of Grace.

You finally wake,
Devoid of false hope of eternity,
They are Dead, their ashes scattered on the ground.
Confined in the perversity of contrived virtues.

That night we stood against the book of dreams.
Holding tight the illuminations of delight.
Harnessing the cries rendered in the real world by
the passionately blessed and anointed.

Lust

It struck me during a
break in the course of one
of those long evenings
of incredible excess
that, counter to the
common view,
you can enter into a State
of Grace with the total
absence and occasion of
sin once you have achieved
balance and moved
to the very
center of lust.

Lust,
Behind and in front of it,
Simultaneously pushed out and upward.
Crossing over all obstacles to moments
of bliss that are total,
Complete,
Absolute in the hour
of your most dramatic
conversion.

You have reached another place that
no opiate ever took anyone.
You are at peace at last.
No world such as this crude one
touching you.

It is striking how despots, tyrants, oligarchs
and thieves have escaped from
here without guilt.

In pristine justification of the
veracity and perfection
of the night.

Dark Underground

Is it a tunnel?
So dim going
down the stairs,
Its break your neck
for certain till
you get to the
thick metal door
that could have come
from the Potemkin.
Now buzzed in and admitted
as member, confidant, brother,
conspirator.

Once across now
definitely outside
a zone of polite
social acceptability.
Real adults the only ones
allowed to play
this game.
Here, unlike most above,
everyone knows
what, why, how,
who they are.

Refreshed without excuses
or social differentiation
this club is for initiates
and those of pure intention.
You serve desire without harm,
not to be lost but
connected through what the
evangelicals, in their
frantic grasp of
delusion,
would declare as an
alliance with,

at minimum, the powers of
darkness themselves.

The truth of it here,
more finely and honestly
tuned than most truth, is
to basic human need.

Truck Driver Girls

At places along the
Road to St Petersburg
Leading North out of town
The small town girls with
Spindly legs stand.
Pathetic creatures mostly.
As far from Night Flight and
Pushkin Square
As the other side of the sun.

Just a few miles out with
What sort of dream I never
Knew but with Truck Driver
HIV rates near 50% in some
Places who knows what theirs
Must be.

Lonely bargain hunters
In cars looking for
Cheap release flow never
Ending to them.
Packs herded in Moscow by
Local pimps and in the
Smaller towns along the
Way reporting in to the
Small town mafia guy to
Shake those pussies down.

And you never saw me out there
Playing that sort of
Gamblers game though
Some do just for a
Perverse thrill.

In love with danger as
Sadly, on some level,
These addict
Girls are.

Looks, Stares, Time

They look directly at you
and stare without aversion.
Hesitation diverted only
by movement.
They resolve the space between
you and them and
keep their distance.
At the same time not
lowering their eyes
like in the West.
Checking, checking, checking
to see what might be there.
Sometimes checking to see
what can be had in a
perilous world where
things change quickly
with little warning
or regard.
They have conquered time
strangely by mostly
disregarding it.
A Russian fifteen minutes
often stretching to
forty five, an hour, more,
sometimes never.
But at least you got your
good long look.

Equivalence

I had a friend there once who
should have known better.
He put himself on another level,
distinct from the girls as if
he was somehow on a
higher moral plane.

Insane it seemed to me at the time.
Demeaning to the whole enterprise.
I saw them as fellow travelers on
another end of the journey.

We together reaching for higher
states of ecstasy.
Safe in the knowledge that, on
the best nights, that the
"whores" and "clients" were
truly and honestly
one and the same.

All together convinced that the
knowing was as important as
the doing.

While, despite the fantasy of
a paid and contrived affair, we
reached for, and at times
achieved, an exultation of
a sort that very few have
the time and courage
to know.

Each of us getting precisely
what we needed from the other.
Without judgment, without guilt.
We renounced that condescending crap.
The vile separation that comes from

thinking you are in a
higher place than
your partner.

Seeking the truth in the core of the night.

Progression:
Her, Herself, Alone

A Fire in Winter

And there it was,
a fire lit to the tops,
all ice and snow bound dreams of
ecstasy.

Finished to the best form you
were absolutely at the pinnacle,
Of the highest order,
Beyond eyes or definition.

Me thinking of or seeing with an
assumption perhaps that I knew all.
Actually seeing nothing till,
at the beginning,
we sat entwined together on
that small red couch.

Speaking volumes all night.
Even with the limits on understanding we had
those days we never were limited actually.

Ever limitless in our knowledge of the other.
Heart wild in chest for you as it has been for so many
others before and since but sublime in the
knowledge and faith in the fact that
you chose me,
Even though the fire
sometimes burned the house
flat around us.

A Walk in the Snow

Then a morning came,
Grey in the low cloud though
Brilliant somehow with a pure light and
New to us,
At least at the very beginning,
of something of rarity.
Special and exact,
We calculated our steps
through a low bank of snow,
Searching for our first rug that
was meant for the summer hallway,
Fresh cut from a bolt in Belgium I think.
Come a long way to Russia that morning
As we had.

Numbers running in close alignment,
First the music of our ages in
Defiance of crude definition,
Then the day and month,
Number of your birthday and
day of our first meeting.

Our numerology marking our path through
the fields of white
stretching endless before us.

Steps still in step as we mark our cadence and
our breath
In the same spirit of that first walk
In the snows of Moscow that stand us well still
As remarkably we stand still together despite
Predictions to the contrary by others and yes,
On occasion,
Even by ourselves.

Beauty

Call me shallow but that
moment I first saw you
blew all assumptions,
of what was seen and what was
possible,
Away to nothing for me.

It was a power of hypnosis
in a glance from you.
It struck me so suddenly,
unaware and mute,
mumbling to myself.

I think you saw me there.
Wondering if I was a
crazy man as indeed
momentarily I was.
Not knowing quite how
to deal with such a
thing.

Experienced and cynical I
thought but not so
apparently.
Immediately caught up
in the force field
which is your
effect on men.

Now and forever
known as victim
number one to
you.

Arrival

When I would arrive,
Mostly at Sheremetyevo,
You would be at your finest.
Top form with warmth, smile,
Full of joy.

Having been parted and
Reunited once again,
Grown even softer
Than before.

Skin with inner luminescence.
Finest posture, attitude,
Carriage.
Every woman's virtue and
Attribute expressed to
Make certain that our difficult,
Good life filled with
Daily frustrations was given
Back to us whole and
Unencumbered.

Strong in each other.
Devoid of those mutual
Afflictions of character
That we never, ever,
Turn on each other.

The Bread of the Gorbushka Bazaar

Walking with you
in the winter city gloom
through the kitchenware stalls,
piles of cheapest Chinese clothing,
hardware,
counterfeit DVD's and
Ukrainian bacon sellers.
We got captured by
the freshest of fresh Uzbek bread,
Thrown up against the convex
oven wall,
given to us seemingly
as one motion.
Pulling it from our pockets
like the very young ones do,
With broadest smile and
full heart.
All for and of each other.
Pulsing with the center and
rhythm of our world.
Together as still it is
between us.

Night Watch

I remember at night,
Looking down from the
ninth floor in
the snow,
Never distracted by
the golden
Armenian dome.

Intense in waiting for
that first determined
glimpse of you
after you
came up from Metro
or, ever so smoothly,
out of a Lada
and up to our door.

It was amazing the
thrill I had,
just a momentary
glimpse sometimes
but enough,
enough my dearest,
In that the first look,
like the latest,
sealed this man
forever.

At the Hall of the Pioneers

Just around the corner from us
it sat centered in a block square
park of its own.
Built in sort of a modernist vein
not exactly Stalinist but not very
warm either.

And we used to walk by regularly,
stopping by the vegetable sellers
at the gate in summer and
sometimes looking up at the
building between the bars.

We would talk of old times and
your own red scarf days in
school where I always
pictured you as the perfect
little girl.

Belting out the Internationale in
your exquisite Russian.
Looking toward the Socialist dawn.
Exactly as scripted from the center
here where the Pioneer prototypes
were forged in purity.
In good health.
Respecting your elders.

Part of the towing of the line.
Believing, as children do,
in not so immutable truths
about the glories of a State.

In its final stage primed for
oblivion and fatally marked,
in the end, by a betrayal.
Not by you my darlings but,

most obviously,
of itself.

When Deadly Night is At Your Door

We were going out from
Metro on a very humid
August night.
Late for us down there
because of the dangers.
After eleven we mostly took
cars.
Better chances even on the street
but this night not for
some reason.

Saw the guy out of the
side of my eye,
On the stair coming up
out near Lesnaya.
Unseasonably but very
well dressed young man
cell to ear.
Typical Moscow bullshit
pose but weird because
of the long coat.

A few steps later noticed
him crossing the street
diagonally after us.
We quickened our step to
almost running.
Now in front of gangster
state bank across Nevsky
to our door.

Electronic key in hand him
lunging after us.
I managed to get my arm
out, pushed him,
Door open, slammed
shut just as he

lunged again,
Me screaming "NYET!"
with the best accent
I could muster.

We were in the elevator
and away and he never got
his weapon out of his coat.
The blood on the street,
That night at least,
Not being ours.

The Girl in the Tunnel

Just near Arbat Metro
It was Spring I think
In one of our typical
Areas to wander near
Our favorite movie, bookstore,
Thai massage place.

We were in the underpass
When you saw the frightened
Asian girl in the grip
Of some street freak,
Dark looking,
South of Russia
Scumbag.

He,
Holding her arm and
Trying to drag her
Off for some nasty
Desire.

Her fear caught your
Eye in this crowded
Place and you
Immediately leaped
Toward this guy like a
Steppe tiger.

Wild thing you were.
Screaming some very
Harsh words that I
Could only feel the
Inflection of.

Telling the girl to
Run for her life.
Then she did.

And we did too!

My breath taken away
By the iron
Determination and guts
Of it all.

My admiration growing
As justifiably as it
Always has since.

Vipers in the Hallway

At nearly four thousand
a month what we got,
outside our very nice
apartment with the
Italian fittings,
was squalor unimaginable
and uproar in the hallway
that frightened you more
than once.

Drug dealing boys indicating
their willingness to bash
each other's heads and,
by extension, murder not
just of their own sprit
but that of poor Soviet
grandma who had lifetime
rights to a prime downtown
location.

Leaching off of her also
crazy old working girl daughter
and very good, sweet
handicapped girl coping
who knows how in that
disordered alcoholic
house.

Us trying to clean there with
limits reached one morning
with piss in a hallway bottle and
on the floor.

We out there disinfecting
in our Moscow high end
paradise.
Finally throwing out all

of their furniture from
the corner of the hall
where their filthy annex had
been set up.

Landlord who knew these
criminals as kids
working with the
cops but only somewhat.

These vipers paying the
local beat guy
we were certain.

So brazen their street
business and the
dirty life lead badly.

Us appalled of course
but somehow fascinated
by the contrast to
the glittering
opulence so
close at
hand.

The Streets Rise Up At Dawn

Imagination never failing the light.
Now so cool and indistinct it hovers
over Lesnaya bringing up the
golden tone.
"Zolotoy" they would say.

From the filthy old facades
churned by many seasons it's
ghostly time in old Moscow
again.

With a weariness of sated desire,
tired from great exertions,
bathed in higher, far higher
levels of physical intensity than
current most anywhere but
here, where the pounding you
take in bed is nothing
next to the relentless
pressure of daily life.

Expanding consciousness spreads
far beyond what could ever
have been envisioned by
daylight.

Moscow River Drive 5:00 AM

How is it that I can still picture
Us in that car,
Winding down the Moscow River road in
The moments just before light.

Calm there after a night of oh so
typical Russian excess.
In quiet observation of the
modality of those most
human dramas,
Without even a shadow of
such between us.

Gently reaching across the
seat to grasp your hand as
I always did there and as
we always walked the
next day to shake
the night off.

Always there if you recall,
Hand in hand, invariably
clasped all over town.

Forever linked there.
Through it all forever still moving,
Always moving within hands grasp despite
and wherever life moves you
Now or with who.

Us triumphant together that way.
That's permanent.

That's how strong that shade is still.

Landscapes

East of Moscow – The Woods

Snow packed so finely in the wood the
black faced fox, his step hardly discernable,
is more silent than the crystals lightly blowing off
the tree, alert fire eye ever waiting.

Are we prowling here or elsewhere again?
Mind filled with rare facility, alert there as nowhere,
Feral perhaps in some sense,
Vision shaped by our own dark walks.

Slowly now, they are a pair, hunting as we thought
they might of necessity, sleep only in the short days,
most wakeful after midnight in that the meal is also
quiet and aware of peril.

Once the ease of movement there belied the starkness,
Cold but sympathetic,
Ever caught by dancing lights though out here
You see it all comes down to stealth at night.

A Place With No Top

No limit, no top,
only endless vertical
hurtling to that low grey
sky up through cloud.

Cries, no tears, no tears
this place can't hear you
anyway they are all
hurtling skyward
themselves with
No limit, no top.

Precisely because there
is no civilized manner
of restraint you can
do, have, see,
screw.

Make it all happen.
Its instant but definitely
not eternal.
Infinite but not endless.
Foolish but not wise.

Even though there is
obviously no God
here there are
Still Newton's
immutable laws of
motion in space and,
Most assuredly,
what goes up must
come
down.

Moscow River Zen

Stoic it seems.
They have no other way
to get through the cold
motionless run of minus
twenty days when the
freeze is such that
even the hardiest of bone
is chilled at the center.

Functioning anyway through
the petrified night air.
So hollow it resonates
sometimes like the
giant ancient bell
that was never hung
from a tower or rung,
Just cracked and stationary
at its perch above the river
that this time of year is not
moving at all.

Solid wind in the drift.
Water turned to dust.
Their gaze the mask hiding
whatever sorrow or turbulence
came to them.
Resolving themselves to
themselves.

They remain in calm discernment.
Not projecting or inflaming you
as a solution or savior or
Resenting your limits and powers
to remove what ails them.

Centuries of training grown
here in the quiet,

in the dark,
by the frozen
stream.

The Towers That Rise From the River

In all lights different,
All weathers,
Atmospheres,
Most variable of places.

Reflection and mutation of shape,
Much of it in paradox,
Exactly the same well over these 500 years.

They brought Italians, of course,
In as designers of the
Red Brick implacable walls.
Moats all filled in now.

On Saturdays they come to
the gardens built in the
space left there.
The brides parties from the countryside,
from backward places,
looking something like
the poorly dressed
overweight hordes
of most any tourist
spot in April or July.

Young hope going toward
New life by whatever
Light is reflected from the
Golden dome,
Or yellow palace wall
Or the facing stones of the
Mausoleum in the square
Or the plaques above the
Bones of long dead
American Communist sons.

Reed and Haywood placed

there in honor
So many a sad Winter
Sunrise ago in that
Light, never the same
and always still
shifting.

A Pulse in the Skyline

What is this burst?
Shaking you up from
the streets.
Leaping like a zealot
into hellfire.

I am caught and released.
Repelled and attracted given
the rigors of the day.
Dealing with every level,
aspect and implication
of the depressing
realities of the
Kleptocratic State.

This is more freedom than
a man can handle.

Anticipation and delight.
You evolve to the highest levels.
These sunset transformations there
empowered to bring on
the ultimate thrill.

The Divinity of the fallen,
The mixed pleasure,
The maximum resource
which is the
night.

Horizon to Horizon

The endless city is never a trap.
Just a pleasure garden of a different sort.
Always bounded by your own desires.
Founded not by nature but against it.

Organized and compounded as a magic elixir would be.
Quite fantastic from pavement to rooftop but
Boundless it would seem as the suburbs are to
their believers.

Those territories when reached are a shock actually.
As if you could divine that the city was indeed infinite.
But that bucolic patch of the outer regions is
not for the likes of us.

Metropolitan and "adventurist" we are, as it
was remarked once and quite accurately
stated after a wise one was
observing us.

Fully deployed in our hazardous playground as
a perfect example of the fact that this
particular merry-go-round is
definitely not for kids.

Boulevard Ring – Twilight 2007

And then in a warmer day the gravel
path on the Boulevard Ring between
Tverskaya and Novy Arbat finally
thawed.

We at last walking with some joy.
Liberated from a half dozen
extra layers or so.
All along the way admiring the
lounging boys and girls.
The very specialness of the way
they have and, for once,
not minding their
cigarettes and
beer cans.

Just now, in half light,
focusing on a glance or
kiss between them.
Reminded that even here,
as harsh as it is,
there are normal kids doing
normal things.

Just so goddamn beautiful.
Beside this you could forgive
them anything anyway.

Now, fully distracted from the
formless gloom of the darker months,
Noticing the subtly waning sunlight again.

New Years Day – The Boys in the Square

They come in their thousands
in their cleanest pressed
winter clothing.
Not in the least minding
the biting wind that
rips across this flat
cobbled space to revel
in their one day of
freedom.

Kirgiz mostly
from that desperate place mixed
with Uzbeks, Tajikis and a
few other self-sorted
immigrant with bad paper
boys.

Exploited but proud
mostly living seven or
eight to a room.
Working every day, seven days,
to get to Western Union
to send every Kopek
that they slave for
back to families,
surely and literally starving
without the aid of these very
good young men.

The reward sometimes is to
be stomped and stabbed by
skinhead Nationalists.
Or, if luckier,
just daily shaken down
in Metro or
in the street
by coward cops

who specialize
in the thousand ruble
sting.

Crossing the Garden Ring

Late night underground the steps down
to the underpass clatter and reverberate.
They bounce from wall to wall diluting
the sounds of other distant steps.
A reinforced feeling of foreboding.
Tense with the possibility of attack.

A more personal extinction not the
least bit farfetched.
Recalling the brief and regular
mentions in the Moscow Times of
folks obliterated on the streets.
Stabbed near Beloruskaya or Komsomolskya or
some such but in the zone and,
near enough to us tonight so that
those thoughts were not a bit fantastic.

All this drama quite real in a manner
recalled from New York in the 70's when
Manhattan was a sewer.
Quite similar then in some ways to this
these days rather than the scrubbed
tourist theme park and crooked
brokers paradise
it is now.

Maybe in fifty years or so Moscow
will become such with most
character and danger stripped
away and just about everyone
but the Wall Street types
playing by the rules.

A Journey, a Bridge, a Town

Far removed from the city I was
lost somewhere in the back country.
Piney woods it seemed,
Great Patriotic War memorials strewn
everywhere as were remnants of the
tank traps the Red Army dug
seventy years before.

Bones there of some of the shattered
millions churned up sometimes.

In the woods they had their holiday camps.
"Shashlik" burning on the grill,
The traditional table laid.

Off to banya in the afternoon and
laying like dead after on
the couch wrapped in a
white sheet.

Them joking about me being passed
out without drinking.
Something I never did there or do of
course while doing everything else and
obeying precious few of your precious
rules being an "artist" without
even a "touch" of irony.

Out from the city, across the bridge,
Away from town and inhabiting another land.

Volga Crossing

We saw him on the opposite bank in
the rickety row boat and, next to him,
A great white dog beginning to breach
The Volga to reach us.

Cresting, so as to carry across in the
May light a hope of passage from
one state to another.
Like Tolstoy he was an espouser of peace,
Perhaps a guru of sorts but complicated like
All Russian things and, strangely, part
Canadian as well.

Not a Holy Man like the Count in the end but
Still a bohemian country "squire" who
Occasionally beat his horses.
He was definitely hiding out from something.

And we needed that Spring,
Like no other,
Born and broken as Winter had been,
Ready to extinguish black,
Unmasked and quite free of the city
and most other things.

The next day you took a picture of me with
"Svo", the same white beast who swam the
Volga after we arrived and adopted
Me shortly thereafter.

City boy come to roost with his great
beauty in the glen.

Spend It All

In my heart and by my
lights they are true
"brothers in arms".
Just plain not caring
sometimes and letting
happen what does.

Throwing themselves headlong,
Crazy actually but
Not insane if you
Know what I mean.

It must have something to
do with starvation.
Lining up for the
simplest of things in
the 40's, 50's,
60's, 70's.
Knowing that really, sometimes,
Grandma really is not having
Enough to eat.

The place was being overrun
Pre-Stalingrad and they
Have all sorts of reasons,
Genetic and cultural that,
I guess,
Could be excuses.

Maybe for them but not for
Me obviously.
Having run off a rail somewhere
Along the line.

Ass end up here in the
Land of the improvident.
Just as happy as could be

Before the money ran out.

Them laughing like the quite
beautiful young lady
lawyer I met early on
who said,
Quite bluntly,
"I'll be your best
friend till you
go bankrupt."

Voices in a Foreign Room

Voices running,
walls collide,
reverberation with
animation and the long way
around every subject.

I understand nothing really,
hardly anything, but you by my
side whispering English phrases
in the pauses.

It is so hard here sometimes.
I can't stand for it.
Not a second longer.

The pounding taken from being
inarticulate hardly needs
explanation.
Certainly not to me who is
filled with the pride of
expression.

Mute unto a kind of living
death without verbosity.
Ego choked with frustration.

A good though involuntary lesson
given with a long overdue
dose of humility.

Run of the Town

We had the license and
We took it.
We had the resources and
We spent what we had.
No fake regret.
No fake piety.
No presumptuous bullshit about
"lessons learned".
You can't resolve it here and
We didn't.
No plea for deliverance and
Definitely,
Most definitely,
No excuses.

This Is Still a Moscow Story

Some say such stories never end and
My part continues of course hearing
those engines, that dull hum above
the Atlantic, taking me back to the
City of my re-birth.

Absent you, there is another tale waiting
for me there that, of course,
will be well characterized in
the minds of others.

Who knows what they will say and who,
Other than me, could possibly care
Less what they think?.

Often evil, sometimes the City of shining eyes and
A good heart, strong limbs and a solid character,
Incredible beauty in all things.

When I see my Moscow from the ground these
are the traits that grab me as this,
then as now, is the town I was
meant to dream in.

Politics, History, Art

Anna

They shot her in the head.
Legs splayed out hallway drenched blood.
Makarov round passed through
And put that hole
in the back elevator wall.
Eventually they put a mirror up
to cover the hole that
I wished Volodya could have
Gazed in.
Becalmed in his evil
When the picked up FSB man,
MVD cops and
Caucuses shooters were
Let go.
In the end not even
A proper show trial
To show the way it was
At our home,
Lesnaya 8,
That Saturday in October
On his birthday.

Motorcade

He rides on.
Infinite, unconquerable,
overarching in his manner.

How direct!
Squinting with his
animal eye directly
at you.

A giant land mass has,
in a sense, committed
suicide and offered up
its own bones to be
ravaged by these
dead eyes filled
with vitality.

The motorcade rolls on
around and out the
Kremlin gate.
Down the broad straight
street leading out of
town to the western
forest lair where
More spoils will be certainly divided,
More bodies most certainly
buried,
More despairs most cleverly
concealed.

This President clearly is for
life now and where is the
likes of Beria at
the end ready to
smother him with a
pillow?

All dead now and not

even such as him around
to stop the madness.

At last,
at the final hour,
he seems immortal and
a true Prince of
Darkness appointed by
acclamation.

And You Thought You Found Your Place With God?

Necromancer,
River of frozen stones.
Place names stuck in the
Grip of the all consuming.

Your virtues are self-control,
restraint, prudence,
an even tempered demeanor,
patience, love.

And then you come to a
Place where none of that
Matters and you can
Cry in buckets,
Beat fist to breast,
Swear eternal allegiance
to your God.

But he's not here brother.
Gone on holiday in the
Crimea or Sochi.
Perhaps he has a place
near Volodya who occasionally
sits down there.

He says he believes in HIM
but how could it be because
by now he's far richer.

So still you persist,
Inside the outer ring,
Searching and publicly
longing for HIM.

So sad to report,
He's gone to ground,
And was seldom,

If ever,
Seen around here
anyway.

The Siloviki

What is behind underneath
and hidden here?
Obscured in layers of a century's intrigues.
Unknowable fact stretching back in
far and near relief.
Depictions in flat planes
without perspective, like
the wall paintings in St Basil's,
But nearer.
As Menacing as a disease in the cells.
Low white blood count and cancerous.
No mercy.

Small and large vampires
stalking these blocks.
Preening in expensive black cars
with blue lights spinning.
Real gangster escort out-riders and duffel
Bags stuffed with
euro and dollar.
Millions thrown like dimes.
No word of honest reality escaping
the permanent inversion
that blankets this
town.

Lubyanka

They pulled Iron Felix down but
He still breathes in those walls,
There on the dread back lit
Forbidden square.

And even though the Chekists
Went to church,
Moved across the street and
got a new name,
I was always at unease there.

Walking near at night I
could hear a Black Maria
Pulling in to the side gate,
Voices, going out from the cars,
lost in the walls of unspeakable
thickness.
I've been told they still keep a
Prison there.

Leon

His shade rises from Red Square
Where he should lie as head of his
first Army.

Rising up like the demon lover of
his brand of the fundamental truth.
In that old time faith he was,
in the end, eternal and
devoid of deviant lies.

And yes, while its true he
conscripted millions and
tried to violently bend
the State to his will he
burned a rare luminous
burn.

He was a founding, guiding, prescient
force for emancipation.
Red flag over a true workers' state.

The Fourth unrealized International not
for the slavery of the gulag.
Not for the glorification of the
bureaucrat.

Clear of mind.
Without a crazy devotion to
the paranoid.

He would have liquidated delusional
states of mind at the top.
Of course, instead, they set out
to kill him.

But they could not terminate the beauty
of the individual emboldened by

workers' solidarity.

Dedicated to the proposition that
we are not alone.
That true unity is at hand with a
hand to grasp.

Red Factory

What was produced here?
Fire, demons, division?
Invocations of another time
The workers march under
The red banner.
Now unfurled to announce
The latest heroic plan
Only to dissolve into
Recrimination, bureaucracy, and
Sullen capitulation.

Not quite what they had
In mind scribbling away
In the British Library
And Berlin all those
Ages ago.

The nature of man being
Un-heroic and anything
But egalitarian
They resorted in their
Frustrations to the
Iron hand and
The Central Order.

Devoted in the end only to
Itself and ridden with a dry rot
No CIA plot could have
Ever dreamed of.
Imploding under its own
Weight and tarring
Progressives the world
Over with the tainted breath
Of decomposition.

The greedy and revolting
Classes of Capital now

Ascending from the dead
Like some horror
Messiahs.

Stealing with impunity.
Making up for
Lost time.
Never again the miracle
Of the workers rising to
Tear their own pain away
And retake history.

The Thread

You are the one thread that
runs through your age and
reweaves the prophets
picture.

Removed from the failure and
distortion of the past.
Distressed and alone,
trusted by none,
respect gone.

You labor on as you
started.
From at least the days
of the Commune.
Those first flags aloft
from 1848 onward to
this day.

The nature and habit of theft
from the people is now
infinitely more complex,
interlaced, global.

Consciousness the world over
May be, just May be,
in the first waking
stage.

Where we, on hold,
wait for the birth of
heroes.
New children unafraid to
shout the truth and
shake the rotten house.

Alive we are with such a

thread, perhaps a shred of
those shredded truths.

Oh to be rising and moving again!

Painter

We were in the old painters
studio, a real garret
packed quite literally
to the rafters
with the work of 1970's Soviet School.
Iron grip post-Kandinsky
20's visionaries craft with hardly
an abstract thought
allowed.

In those days, your coveted
place was secure in the
"House of Artists" where
American decadents
like a Pollock
with his unhappy
sneer and
rebel stance
would not have
found space
anyway in a place
where the rule of realism
was not that real.

Leave it to the NY school
to redefine things.
Besides our old friend was
actually very good and had
done views out the window with
the same perspective
as the view from ours.
It's a work we bought and still own
that sat in Moscow long
years waiting for
a exit permit,
a bit of drama and
a poem.

"Leosha"

Alexey stands as a Tsar would stand
But has no mace, no sword, no pointed dagger,
But words, words in sharp burst
Shredding a smoke filled lyric night.
The verse there, as always, in
his mother's basement club.

Outside, the streets of Kitai Gorod filled
with drink and loud denials while down
those stairs the guitar sound was
Cutting the smoke now with ballads of the
Frozen Stream.

Desperate mixed Jewish and Slavic love songs,
Misplaced and longing as the sellers
Stand, in cold air,
Plying the old style Russian
Trade of heart and tongue
In Kievsky Vokzal hard by that
River that carries that
Word and world away.

Maximalism

Right up to the limit,
Over the top,
Exactly as you like it.
The maximalist never is
Imbued with the concept
Of consequences.
Just being for the
Extremity of the position
Was his justification.

That the excess is
Self-sustaining.
That being over is
Far better than under.
That all roads lead us
To him and him alone.

Here it's the expression of purest
Ego only a youth would even
Try to pull off.
Wheels still spinning
Even after the inevitable
Crash and the sober
Admonishments have been
Rendered meaningless by
The bold defiance completely
Realized by this boys
Convulsing heart!

Mayakovski

The kids drink beer
and play at his feet.
Oblivious mostly to
his lineage and fate.

As a Futurist he would
probably have been amused.
As a Bolshevik less so.
Shocked I think by the
imperatives of today.

Strange Things,
I-Pad, Pod, Phone along
with whatever other clutter
is swept up from the internet
and dumped in the street.

The revolutionist in him would
have picked up this stuff and
run with it like an
Egyptian in an Arab Spring.
The first one to point to
something fresh.

He would, I think, pull down
his own fine statue here
that we passed by in
all weathers which is still
the May assembly point for
what remains of the
true believers.

On the real workers holiday the
voice is resonating with
the echo of the full throat
of a poet in the real world.

Urging on the ultimate victory then,
"done with life",
rotten with contradiction,
shooting himself one April
not even able to
walk in one last
parade.

Yesenin in the Lobby Bar of the Angleterre Hotel

I could imagine him sitting
here this morning slouched
in his chair.
Hands quivering and
chin all a-twitch.

He, cold after a three
day binge.
Me, giving him some "fatherly"
advise and
He, with a "fuck you" half
Smile as he tried to
assemble himself once
again for an inspired
assault on a
day.

And of course the advise
not taken he would
return to his rooms
and continue raging at
Isadora.

Up there, on the fourth floor,
the blood red moon and
the unfair nature of
a transient spring.

As such the rope didn't end it.
It continues with this music in
the streets of St Petersburg.
His beauty is of no end for me.

I sing my own song of him and
all the lost brothers
down the years.

I sing a "Song of Myself" and of
time and of you my love.
Here this morning in Russia alone
in the lobby with a
dream.

The Broken City:
Disorder in the New Town

Moscow Minus 21

Its minus 21 tonight in Moscow baby and
the frost over frost is piled
high on Lesnaya.

Drunks at risk of hypothermic demise.
Blind, perhaps unwitting, not like us
with eyes wide open,
Staring into a lapse of heart and
nerve when compared to that
instant understanding, that spark,
that set us on this road those
long years ago.

In an even colder time it was now
the warmest of winters.
Strong and certain as you were
as a girl.
But woman now this climate closed
in on us.
These lapses beyond contrition it seems.

But there, in the ice preserved, on Lesnaya
At minus 21 tonight,
All human aspiration and faith waiting
For our return.

Jealousy

Ravenous,
The beast defeats time and
cowers in the brain like
Cancer,
Devouring sense and
rendering rational thought
in tatters.

It heaves,
Like a seizure would.
Contorting thought to twist
upon itself and render you senseless.

What state this is you do not know.
It blooms like kudzu in the southern summer,
Covering over the contours of what used
to be a fairly good mind with the
twisted vine and strangling root of
something like the totality of
despair.

Somehow, you rise to cut out the
heart of the vine.
You rise to calm the torment which
is yourself and
learn to think
again.

Sleep

No sleep it seems forever,
When exhaustion transcends this desire,
Just longing for repose,
Absence devoid of peace.

No sleep tonight baby no dream.
It won't be forever but this is out of time,
out of character.

There is a hormone or chemical for
this somewhere out of balance I think.

Where is the night?
Is it forever without rest?
What is it?

No sleep, no sleep tonight
baby till I pass out
from here and learn
to breathe
again.

Trans-Siberian Blue

And now is the time of
Reflection dearest dear
As darkness is finding
Early light.

A moon sets across the steppe tracking
The nomadic trail of the old Magyars.
We discovered there once we had a slight
Streak of the same blood.
Alma-Ata trackless waste to Budapest.
My grandfather standing in the station there
Looking to America,
Yours to Moscow and the glory of
Red Square.
The old Commissars horses pounding
Foot to stone.

Connection rising, rising in
Our blood and body.
As once we were at once connected seemingly
Forever but now as metaphor for
What was and could have been under
A moon on the steppe at
Midnight.

Twilight of the Patriarch

I wish I could have been
"Daddy" this and "Daddy" that.
The authority on all things as your
leader, hero.

A pillar of whatever community you
may have had in mind.

But that's just not me baby!

As still a free form dreamer and carrier of
various unreformed flames of
long dead movements.
Discredited in a resurgent right wing time.
Though somehow now credit remains in
the hearts of many who were there.

Those girls struggling for your
liberation before your birth.
My first long dead girl first
amongst them.
Fighting those patriarchies to
the death.

A struggle for a freedom you
found constricting.

Finding yours now in an
order and regularity lost
to my senses too
long ago to
retrieve.

Adventurers

"Iskateli Priklyucheniy" they would have
called us.
Walking hand to cheek as a
Whisper given close in confidence down
Tverskaya in all weathers.

Firm of step and action and
also full, absolutely at the
top of life.
Caught there with the motion of
life itself.

I prefer to see us in your sisters words.
Ringing in memory pronouncing us "matched".
Caught up in adventure then despite
the obvious "miss" that
some could see.

Always in our eyes together.
Fingers intertwined at a cellular
level it seemed.
Those days not a shadow of a
flicker of a doubt.

No thoughts then of the defiance of
the "natural" order,
The disapproving gaze of others,
The stirring of the un-conceived shouting
of genetics and delay.

None of this!

Just the two adventurers on their
path across time.
Outside of time itself and in
mind's eye eternal.

When You Know Just What You Are

Some say they are born that way.
Sprung from a clean Midwestern soil
like your new paragon perhaps.

Others we find must evolve on their
own Galapagos of struggle and pain.

All this I know now.
And wiser still am climbing up the
chain from mollusk to chimp.
Slipping down the rocks near the shore.
Covered in a primordial ooze.
The unicellular building blocks of
life impeding me.

I struggle on.
Just clear of one delusion then
clouded by another.
Just reaching one plateau only to
have to learn who I was when faced
with the sheer rock wall of
grief that was losing you.

Now learning even more on the climb up
that rock face to my own peculiar and
quite secular sacred space where
I know I must leave you to
your own devices and
desires.

Nights in Calm Reflection

Receding from me now the night of
stark terror and the four AM panic
that knocked me off the rail as
surely as a stroke or
embolism would.

This was of the heart and spirit and
of the realization of the absolute
waste of it all when neglect and
willful disregard met the hard
and implacable shade that is
your character direct from
your father.

Literally so, he's the Holy Ghost not
resident with us but as a shade and
specter both familial
and deeply rooted.

All these types of things are in the
Nature of us both my dear,
Which somehow accounts for estrangement
Without betrayal.

For now there is separation in love and service.
I'm still without anger and you still
my closest friend.

Sitting up here still without you.
Still, my dearest, alone.

Lost beside this door and looking to
the balcony for the Spring Flowers.

Only the bare concrete and the Sun awaits me now.

Traces

I found the Kazakh Tenge on the floor,
All shiny bright like gold but
Base metal of course.

It was from that last trip home for you I guess.
It's placed high up on the shelf,
Far away and hidden so I can't see
it now or ever.

Burning me,
Its brilliance shining
through like your words.

Words which sometimes held such insight.
Words looking right through to the core.

So searing and bright that all the
emotion and essence and
overriding strength we had,
The dead certainty in each other,
Could be blown down like a broken and
abandoned Yurt.

Now like an old tale from home.
Un-tethered and destroyed in a
blizzard out there long ago
in the harsh weathers.

Buried under the thick skins of
your ancestors.

May the River of Life Flow Through You

As it struck like a revelation this
well of feeling was stranger after pain,
Stronger after suffering,
As basic as compassion and how
easy it may be to drop that
part of the chain.

"I'm going to be selfish this time!"
And true enough as that notion goes,
But life conserved is life preserved,
As I now, in certitude,
Know it.

It lies before me as I now reveal it to
Myself and others,
As I now see the prior road and
After as resolution banishes doubt and
The spirit rises in me.
Not holy in any way but very old none the less.

This is the river I have sought.
This is the stream denied and now found.

Without Gods or Prophets to guide me but as
Certain and guided by truth as if they were.

Nighttime and the Idealist

In dead of night the idealist is still
reaching for the dream as
the realist is counting up the
sums.

Add, subtract, decide,
That's the way those accounts
build up while out on the
promontory the wind whips
the dreamers face and
hard rain lashes out at
his skin.

There exposed for all to see while
more patient games continue on
their stately and implacable
path toward stability.
The lightness of being born from
knowing exactly where
the money is.

Out front the owls are sounding their
call to the seekers in the wood,
All unbalanced with poetry in their eyes,
While deep in the eucalyptus grove the
Bard sings of the warmth of summer and
the biting cold that comes fast after
Fall to the improvident
few distressed by excess,
Vision and the lure of
Abstraction.

The Light in the Eye

There is a light that shines within.
I see it clearly now,
Not baseless or immaterial but
Of the now.

The pure substance of what is
Built in the world and what
Can pass between the two,
Locked in an embrace.

So it is with a power in us still
as I sit on an opposite side of
Planet One,
Our one and only home.

I did this to myself I guess to
have to build again but was told
just today about the light in my
own eyes and understand the strength
within that others see
so clearly and,
Without dismay, resolve to be
more than just a retinal
reflection of a time
with you that came
but is no more.

On the Nature and Occasion of Sin

Some have taken note that the concept
of "sin" is a serious business not
to be toyed with by such as us,
But, oh baby, do we ever know our sins and
the occasions thereof!

Though the "pie in the sky" crowd would
wail over theirs ours, I think,
are indeed a more serious matter.

Long on contemplation, short on revision,
venal mostly, and against ourselves almost
Always.
Not even against each other though there
are those who do say exactly this that,
"Your best friend would not have done that to you."
At least not with "him" and not "quite" that
way though they just don't "get" the
circumstance and the complications.

Times like that night of your long tears and
My own "near death" experience,
Brought on more by foolishness than
Sin and the utter seriousness of what
We still are to each other,
Even unto death.

Night Lounge Delhi

Global again the artist waits for
transport and hope.
Sleepless for once out of necessity.

The steepness of the learning curve still
evident as was hope itself once before it
seemed the darkness came and all was
extinguished.

As midnight met doom as light failed and
contracted into the pinpoint of a black hole.
The irony of infinite energy concentrated,
The physics of less than nothing.

Far past the breaking point,
Forever it seemed to him,
Far past, Far more than he ever
thought he could endure.

Our godless spirit merged as it
Always has and will do in
Eternity as we walk this
Loop together as you,
Angel, my dear one,
Will forever know.

Not enough my brilliance or your
Infinite capacity for insight.
Not enough the overwhelming emotion of
Our beginning and a wonderful string of
Days and years,
Not enough my dearest,
Not enough for you.

Lives of Magic

Is it possible to live each moment in the light,
With wonder and a heart so full of desire and
Magic that every instant is alive,
Scintillating with a vibrancy and
Fullness beyond limits of mere
Description?

Can we be where hyper-awareness meets deepest sleep,
Where acute intellect crosses over to fire creation,
Where myth and symbol mix with the history of cognition?

Man dances his greatest dance in the fineness of
an arc of paint,
A line of dialogue,
The bite of lyric and deepest song.

Being there is often enough where art
crosses with a child, his handprint
on the museum wall as he stares up,
Eyes wide,
Indelibly seeing at once and forever.

That's where the voice from the center
Rises and all the lifeless prose,
An emptiness justified as "process" and "order",
Is swept to sea by what we know as true callings.

The wonder and the magic that in the end makes
Earth habitable and life a greater thing,
The greatest thing that is when death is
Banished and work that lasts is standing.

Outlaws

Not brigands exactly but outlaws none the less,
We joined up against them to bash away at pain and
Find a grail outside their rules and norms and
Evening sung devotions.

For a while this worked just fine and set our
Love to task,
Without a thought for consequence we went our
Way, ourselves alone,
Distinctive in the pleasure took with losses
Hardly any and in the main we left behind
Only pleasure, never guilt or fear or even
a hint of that sterile despair I
had fled to Moscow from.

It seemed we beat them at their game but
came the day of our return to a "City on a Hill",
The land of Puritan toil and virtue as reward that
was always waiting there to sit on my neck.

Arms outstretched to greet us as the whiff of
corruption attached itself to pure intentions.

You saw the dire consequence here for those who
stray and stumble.
Just a short step off their track,
An error in judgment, a "few" bucks short and done.

Your conversion was remarkable, swift and true and
to be on the path in freedoms trail must be a
Revelation.
And while I wish you well and
All due steadiness and speed,
As the days pile up and those virtues
Multiply just give a thought now and
Then to an outlaw heart still beating,
Still working hard and raging on.

Cost

And what does it cost us in the end?
Our devotions to concepts and
perceptions that sometimes
devour our senses and
present us with "too many"
choices.

In Loss, devoid of qualities like
endurance, steadiness and faith.

By which, of course, I mean faith in
another who holds us in arms,
brushes our hair and
makes us whole again.

Such belief undermines all doubt and
erases regret at choices made and
adhered to with a love that is
defended, struggled for even,
Held close to the end and not
allowed to expire in a pool of
projections about what is
"supposed" rather than known.

All now revealed in light and
not imagined in shadow or
distorted through the
prism of fear.

Being steadfast is not counting the cost,
Being true not caring about it.

Images in Another Night

Grey, the color of Winter,
Dark my thoughts tonight which
should be brilliant and
descriptive of your beauty
and intellect.

Pale, receding instead from
that incipient tremor from
you I noticed on the
screen through that camera.

You, some distance away from me now.
In another man's space where alone
you sit waiting for what I don't
know of or understand.

An alien touch from another landscape.
From regions unknown to me.
From across that strangers world where,
And how could it be,
A stranger does indeed sit between us.

This no taller than the first grass grown
up in this season when compared
to the endless fields of
shimmering beauty and
sea of green that carried
our love across the lands and
down rivers teeming with life.

Whole oceans of us that I saw just yesterday,
Flickering on that screen in your eyes and
Reflected in the small tears seen
When I spoke of Moscow, light
And Springtime.

Fate

It seems as if we make our own.
Finely drawn blank upon the page.
All set, as in the cheaper dramas,
novels, plays.

All such with protagonist,
dramatis personae, sets and
all devised by our own foul
hand as if a torture room was
set to music.

The screams from there are of
the opera chorus below the
battlement basement walls in
small, small rooms.

Why is it so for us?
Native optimistic tones are
played and looped from
childhood forward by so many others in
a drift of fortune easy, fine and
driven to the expression of
excellence and light.

I have seen such, well brought up and
groomed for glory and while I
myself was never one and
never could be I see just
the faintest chance that the
latest fated blows have
glanced off this tender son.

That slow learning can sometimes equal slow healing.

My Lost Poem

Scattered everywhere it seems from
Putney to Novosibirsk.
Lost by the side of the road mostly,
Early on, in the throes of alcohol and
Foolish unrequited loves.

Later on through purely mildness and
Selfish deposits of self-inflicted pains I
Guess but their voicing didn't fade,
Even the ones caught in the great
1972 bonfire where in a post
Midnight fit of inebriated madness,
Willfulness, perversity years of
Not so bad but immature work was
Incinerated in pursuit of the best as
Down through the 70's when things just
Played themselves out.

It was in the beginnings of my negligent
Emotional separations from you that the
Paradox reappeared.
Way down in the later start of a new century.
All-in, the thread renewed.

It was your face, spirit, love,
Still without time or limits to
Me that bore this fruit and
Our sweet burdens forward to
This magnificent day.

Open City

There we were, scanning romantic
lyrics and country idylls caught
in the act of creation.

How uncharacteristic of me being so and
how you noticed as the space between us
lessened and we progressed.

Then you said you had "changed" and I guess I
did as well but it too may pass away unless
tended and I know now what preserves me.

To keep, nurture, love, hold each
shining second without such
dissonance.

All slips away and the distance
between us brews with cold and
forbidding diversions in
storms and hurricanes of
breakdown and
disturbance.

Who thought of rebirth and
second chances was thinking
of me!

As anthemic moral choices dance in my eyes,
The sum of self rises and you defy
The fathoms to join me.

Job One

My best ahead of me,
toil is joy and work lifts me
up like a prince or master of
my own devise.

Independent and free of the stress of the task.
Never ill-considered and under conceived.

In you I found it and in you I conspire at
last to be myself alone.
Without the influence and distraction of suffering.
Devoid of doubts and struggles.
Clear headed and full of purpose.
Directed outward not inward.

Developed and fine honed,
With specific intent to be of service to
Life and love.

The focus finally where it can do some good.
Not for me alone, it's you my love,
Descended from the far off tribes,
Come off a plain so distant yet so
Close to me.

Alive in colors discerned in the glow of a crescent,
Far off in the East and always present as
Life beats in my chest and your hand
Rests there calmly at last.

Home At Last

Will You Walk This Way With Me Again?

Here we are today devoid of artifice at last.
In the time of admission and justice where
what was lost is weighed against
what we have to gain.

At last and completely we walk together,
all of a piece, hands intertwined,
not a step out of place or
out of time.

Assured in the perfection of what is
in sync as opposed to the mostly
ill perceived notion of what
is not.

All deceit put on balance and the traces
of betrayal placed exactly where they
need to be, which is behind us always
in that we were always together though
separated by a generation or more in
the literal sense.

Actually most acutely proximate and
aligned as in the motion and
rotation of planets.

Our orbit in the light and shade of the
burning of the white hot sun of
passions gates wide open
to us once again.

The Window (Moscow Slight Return)

And I was there in May on the rebuilt block,
The study room window open to the air,
Wind drifting down Lesnaya as it
does softly on weekend afternoons.

Girls floating on the corner,
their laughs drift up to the
open space others inhabit now.

The spirit there is us between us as
always it hovers in these rooms.
Permanent and resolved, basic as
understood by all with eyes and
hearts and a comprehension of
what came to us.

Those few short years ago, we entered
those long long seconds where the
devoted look up together as the
longest ray of afternoon light
shines on the face of the
beloved.

You, the found one, the no longer lost.
Me, among the saved who are without distress.
Now emerged from a long night in winter to
the longest days of the year.

Walking again on Lesnaya where a sun burns at
Midnight and the light pushes dread
aside while hands that grip for
life itself move darkness
back and away for
good and all.

The Streets near Tverskaya

As the morning crowd began to swell in
Metro and the freshly washed pavement
was sparkling with those golden speckled
droplets that only the dusty morning
light here produces,
I found myself drawn,
on my early walk today,
to those side streets where
we used to walk together.

Close together, in all weathers,
Hands so tightly bound that we were
like Chang and Eng,
those long ago Siamese Twins,
It seems we were as spirits,
One on one on one as one.

Incredible as it is now to me on this trip alone.
Walking back in mind's eye to those days and times.
Days absolute and special to us now re-committed as
the reality of who we are together came rushing back.

The time of bonding here in this crazy house of a city where,
for us at least, a kind of purity and a singleness of
joint purpose were absolute, complete and as
whole then as it is again today.

When You Are Young and Filled with Wonder

The streets reverberate and all is heightened sensation,
lust, devotion, ideals all mixed as you stroll at dawn.

Not a worry or even a hesitant moment.
Straight forward and not diverted by or
deterred by circumstance.

That's the essence I try to capture for myself.
Well and long past it as I walk these streets renewed,
Without a moment of delay and aware at mirrors
glance that time these days is indeed of the
essence for me.

Striding this foreign path,
feelings raw and heightened once again by
strangeness though never out of place.

Never dull or frightened like some might be.
Happily gone and landed in this Martian
landscape where ass-backwards is so
twisted that its straight.

There are only left turns off this road.
Good American Boy gone bad in Russia again.

Fidelity and the Greedy Eye

And what is real and what is not?

Essential information actually this
morning on the street where the cars
are hurtling, plunging over-fast down
the hill toward the Kremlin and
everything is being sold and so
few things conserved.

And you might ask how can such
goodness and sweetness of heart
and action seen here sometimes
survive?

I would have to honestly say that the
good survive with great difficulty.
Imbued with the spirit of fidelity.

Overcoming somehow greed and
the fear of lost souls.
Lost indeed here as in a charnel house of
the truly damned and those who
found theirs somehow treating them
as the precious things they are and you,
Uncharacteristically for such a place,
with the respect yours deserves.

The Picture

When it arrived from Moscow the story ended and
started in the same blue late twilight,
Very early night that he captured that day.

Ambiguous as always as light flew across the
lands of Europe and the seas to us,
Representational in the mid-distance as
was the "Vokzal" and in the nearest
aspect of the dome of the Armenians.

Just next to Metro and those stairs where
our hearts often met trudging up to
ground level to take our place
on the horizon.

And where does the scene take us now
and where are we bound?
Voiced as the folk-singer now in
his seventies once sang as a
youngster in another town where
the bards roam and the winter of
1961 was also cold but not
quite of this.

Our scene now hangs in our home along with
Our first breath together and with us,
The story never over,
The shapes shift to their next
Level as shadows play on
A freshly painted wall.

Coda:
Last Visit To A Dark Town

Into the Grey, Moscow, February 2013

And, after some months away,
You descend blindly once again
Down from the cloud where
Just a moment before you were
surrounded by light,
Down, as far as you can
Fall without a fatal bounce, or,
Perhaps, a rebound of sorts.

They wait for you there, the
Profoundly concerned and the
Hyper-aware, with ancient
agendas that even you,
Older now with that critical
mass and weight of experience,
Can hardly apprehend.

Why is it that the fascination remains?
Why is it that a tragic history and
the extremes of beauty,
duplicity, faith, charity,
murderous intent,
the totality of utter concealment
combine here to ensnare the
imagination and render
the tranquility of home a
dull and sullen refraction
as a static and 'so called'
democracy?

Moscow cloud, devoid of even
the slightest variation or remittance,
dangerous, vexing,
Driving me very clearly and definitely
to the airport and away again
only and certainly forcing a
return to marvel at the power

that even an initiate
can hardly resist and never
long endure.

The Order of the Line/Embassy Dawn 9:00AM

As a dancer is caught flat without shoes
wandering baseless and etched
not flesh more stone as
The funnel cloud bends down its conical,
The reverse on the Veldt
as a long necked beast
that swoops in to devour,
despoil, render unto who?

Perhaps a mere mortal this time.
Someone with both cash and determination,
sinew and stealth.
You Come Down on Us
You Swine.
Bearing your shine
as well as your teeth!

So much money in your pockets
the bulges show as you put us
on the block to be sold
down south to work a cane field
or airport or bank.

I would sing the Internationale tonight
but my Russian is bad
and you are all asleep.
I'll dream instead
a rare and fanciful dream
of cowering revolution
in the drawing rooms, universities
and libraries.

No hope of workers rising here!
No hope of redeeming this coupon
given in blood and good faith
but worthless in the face of
the grab, the hustle,

and the perfected for all time
confidence game.

Noontime Dom Knigi

That Saturday
As we emerged grumbling
from the passage
up to street level there
was no excuse for them.
Once again
Behavior so execrable, unforgivable,
Vile.

Devoid of common sense,
drunken,
never sober
from the night before.
We had had it with them.

We crossed over
Seeking refuge in the bookstore,
largest in town,
a place of learning
of some renown.

Walking the aisles of poets,
novelists, artists
and scientists
of all kinds
we recovered in their presence
as those few of feeling do
in this town that
doesn't need your tears
doesn't return love
doesn't give a centimeter
Back.

It was then that
the trick worked us.
Showing an angelic face
at Noontime.

A line of seraphim
waiting for
an Autograph.
Their very own author
of fancies.
Not taking notice
not even for a second
of the noise
and fury
of the gathering hordes.
Their gangland style.

This place is a monster.
Deceit mixed with all
forms of human greatness.
They,
well concealed
within their own
parallel lines.
Being drawn down
from soul.
Perfectly human.
Wild,
Strange,
Ungovernable.

Gulag

They tried to bend me down,
Rivers of pain, drool,
abscesses there festering
with their fabrications,
Lies innumerable to assure
that I'm all done in here.

I can imagine how it happens,
to be trapped by both your
own and others devices.
Where harm and blame,
enough to go around,
comes to rest and it all
being settled upon you.

Guilty on the margins but
not in the facts.
Distraught and distracted but
always more, never less,
than concise and actual in
your own accounts.

But it was no matter there.
They in their judgment shining on.
A bright future ahead for them without
the slight tremors of hand or lip
that betray the unconvinced.

Straight up! All lies!
Not a care in the world for
you and your messy,
imprecise veracity.
All gone down to the hanging on
the cusp of dawn.

You, out on the borderlands,
Paying any price to slip across,

Great courage and going through
side by side with your partner.

Them, frustrated in the end.
Their character to look for a
cringing soul all befouled
by fear.

The Door of the Ukrainian Cafe/
Guli: April 2013

And you were there, in the
hour before light
framed in the door.
And though we were still there
under deadly threat you
decided our freedom in a glance.

Warm,
Your face shows the way of the world.
All turbulence put and set aside.
My life, my peace, what can you
do but stand beside me.
Glue, you are what holds.

As they were stalking us days before
in Metro we knew we knew
what fear was.
But here,
this late, late evening song
is what defined us and
as it was there as your
brightness of eye defined the
room.

I will never see days such as those.
Clod field passing by.
Borders closing in on us.
Hell on us.

Always, my darling I will see you.
Always with the definition of the light holding
you as you pass through that door.
Carrying a bag but no baggage.
Going through the chaos and away from the dark.
Finding me there under the sky in a cold
Spring Night.

Driving Naked

That spring finally deposited us
in a strange land.
Corrupted to be sure as
all such places are but
filled with fresh and
honest love.

We saw it at once on the street
all hands intertwined
looking straight and true.
None of that grasping,
few if any sharks cruising this
poor but wealthy
inland empire.

After freezing all winter,
near death in the city,
their sweetness turned our
hope around.

Still running to be sure.
Still looking for the
footfall of doom.
Still under another name.
But somehow here practically
unafraid.
Liberated and cleansed in the
enchanted air.

Not exactly driving naked
and free but hopeful
at last.
One short bolt of courage away
from leaving Moscow
in memory.
Not to return this lifetime
perhaps.

Leaving this territory through
fairyland.

Borders

This time last year as we
made the final border we
looked one to the other
in disbelief.
Lost as we had been we
never lost sight of the
other and that strength
that went over with us.

Sometimes waivered or just waved
through we crossed resolute and
hid our fear.
Without the slightest doubt or
cowards hesitation we
looked straight ahead and
right in their dirty eyes.

The spring trees burst their winter
tightened buds and waves of pollen
roared across those old
seized lands of war.
We surged as well and tightened our
grip and took nourishment and
moved smartly and correctly.
Beat them at their own games good and proper.
Got the hell out of there to home.

The Old Traveler

Lost here America all fathers fall I'm
Falling back to Russia all over and across that
Line I always cross the crosshairs planted on
Me as old Volodya's dead eye blinks on
The slipshod and crooked path,
Longing to take me down that sun splash of
Boulevard and those streets around the
Station we walked daily.

Never end,
They will themselves be in me and
Through me tonight.

Alive,
Moving on my Tverskaya nerve ending
Unendurable fascination of the distraught and
Stoic temperaments not to be conveyed to that
American fantasy where safety is a premium,
Them laughing their asses off at our
Caution and prudence.
We are a joke to them.

And the uninitiated call it a romance
As the older hands reveal
What really is in store for you good
Western boys when you delay that ride and
Fail to sail.

The sound of Moscow and its smacking lips
As it grips your feet and drags you down,
The pull of Moscow ever after,
It's rare rough being always alive.

Eye all afire with it forever.
No matter where,
No matter where,
You are not the same.

Three Years Out – Moscow – Day and Night

And just when winter departed it returned as
thoughts of Russia ran all night in concert
with the long fought desire to leave that place
As freshly broken,
The past rises up.

Moscow never ending always enduring never
sleeping always pulsing under frozen ground.
The surface expands to encompass all of it,
The broken parts as important as the whole.

Bodies fluoresce as in the shining deep
the lights in the eyes erase judgement.
As the dust blows down Tverskaya in August,
And all is run down to the ring of inner glories,
As one false move extinguishes the other.

All rise up in the obliteration,
And your Moscow never stood for its instance on
The hardness of harsh reality and a lack of pity,
Never refraining from comment and reference to
itself and the compulsions of the masses.

Deep love develops for black hearts and frozen mud,
Thin soup, violence, all forms of cruelty mixed with
this long debated fineness of spirit,
This mystery poignant and vital that binds there
eternally one to the other.

Blame it on all that fucking beauty,
Blame it on all that fucking.
The strangeness that is this addiction
challenging survival.

And that crude beast of a city itself will
never unravel as it logically should,
As we all should be ready for some

form of an undoing in preparation
for the January doldrums.

And why false heat?
And why amber diffused twilight
below the Baltic shore?

Overloaded, the great ship drifts down
the river like a Scandinavian trader of
long breezes,
Of millennia berserk in the stillness
of what fullness they knew.

There they sit preserved,
Hidden in the peat with chain Mail,
Dull bespoke instruments of torture,
Eyes out and materials transmitted all
Down generations.

Still, us ruminating on the side streets,
Walking, endlessly moving down the
Pereuloks and Prospekts,
Dead ringers for the lost,
Unconsumed by false knowledge.

As sleeplessness forms its battalions,
Never seen or apprehended but ever
Shifting as the day there blends to night,
And the live stream plays endlessly through
Till dawn.

John Huey
December 2015

Glossary

This Glossary encompasses mostly Russian words, people, place names or terms that are not fully defined in the body of the poem. Many of the definitions contain my own comments and/or opinions. Further information on all of this is available in Google Search or (in English or Russian versions) on Wikipedia.

Anna: see Politkovskaya, Anna

Aptecka: Russian Drug Store

Armenian Dome: 19th Century Armenian Church in Moscow directly adjacent to the
Lesnaya Street Exit of the Belorusskaya Metro Station.

Babushki (plural of Babushka): The real Russian heroes. Best grandmas ever. No Russia without them.

Banya: Traditional Russian bath house/sauna. Can be public or private.

Belorusskaya: 1948 Metro Station built below and connected to a 19th Century Train Station of Victorian design and the same name in Moscow.

Beria, Lavrenity, 1899-1953: Head of the NKVD Secret Police organization during WWII and Stalin's right hand man thereafter. Shot in the basement of Lubyanka after Stalin's death in 1953 on Khrushchev's order. Legend has it that he may have hastened the death of Stalin in his final hours.

Boris: see Yeltsin, Boris

Boulevard Ring: Moscow Inner Ring road. Old, wide boulevard split by a park running its length in its center. Developed between the 1790's and 1820's. Fine statue of the poet Yesenin is here mid-way between Tverskaya and Novy Arbat.

Chekist: Member of the Cheka, first Soviet Secret Service 1917-1922, founded by Felix Dzerzhinsky (see Iron Felix). Commonly used to name current and past members of successor Security organizations, NKVD, KGB, FSB etc. "Once a Chekist always a Ckekist!"

Cherkizovsky: Largest bazaar in Russia and largest market of any kind in Europe closed in mid-2009. Famous for low prices, "grey" market Chinese goods and illegal foreign workers. Azerbaijani owner lost this business despite being close to former mayor Luzhkov due to a falling out with Putin and the rising tide of politically motivated anti-immigrant/nationalist sentiment.

Coffee Mania: Very pricey, high quality European style coffee shops/restaurants branches of which are now all over central Moscow.

Commune: 1871 Socialist uprising in Paris quickly overthrown and brutally put down by the French Army.

"Crazy Town", "Sumashedshiy Gorod", "Сумашедший Город": aka Moscow

Dom Knigi: Novy Arbat branch is Moscow's largest and most comprehensive bookstore that holds frequent author events and readings. Foreign language as well as most all Russian books are available here.

Droog: trans. Male friend.

Face Control: Strict Moscow Nightclub entry requirements based on appearance and perceived wealth. Think Studio 54 on steroids.

Foreigners sometimes given a "pass" but not always.

Fourth International: International Communist Organization founded by Leon Trotsky in 1938.

FSB: Federal Security Service, successor to the KGB that combines CIA and FBI type functions. Putin's home outfit.

Garden Ring: Second major ring road in central Moscow. Eight lanes with no divider in many places. Jammed always. Can only cross on foot using underpasses which are everywhere in Moscow.

Golden Ring: Golden Ring Hotel, four star hotel in the center just off the Garden Ring, near

Stary Arbat and the Foreign Ministry. More Russian than International in style with fewer foreign guests than other establishments at this level.

Gorbushka Bazaar: Very interesting outdoor market next to the Gorbushka electronics sales complex outside central Moscow. At Bagrationovskaya station on the Moscow Metro Red Line.

Gorky Park: 300 acre park in Moscow and the most famous in Russia. Gorky Central Park of Culture and Leisure opened in 1928. Reconstructed in 2011 as a more eco-friendly free park with most amusement park type attractions removed.

Great Novgorod: See Veliky Novgorod

Great Patriotic War: How Russians always refer to WWII.

GUM: High end now redeveloped shopping complex built between 1890-1893 directly on Red Square. Cold War photos seen frequently in the West in the 1950's - 1960's showing Russians standing in long lines to buy day to day goods not readily available elsewhere were often photos from GUM.

House by the River: aka "House on the Embankment" was purpose built in 1931 to house the families of the Soviet governing elite. It's estimated that during Stalin's purges of the mid to late 1930's that over 700 residents here were liquidated.

House of Artists: Central House of Artists was a Soviet institution for State sanctioned (Union of Artists of the USSR) and affiliated artists. Still in existence as a large exhibition and artists space across from Gorky Park and attached, in the same complex, to the modern Russian art collections of the New Tretyakov gallery.

Internationale, The: Song embraced by Socialist revolutionaries (in many different versions) worldwide with the original French version dating from 1871. Still the anthem of the Communist Party of Russia. Russian version begins, trans. "Stand up, ones who are branded by the curse, All the world's starving and enslaved!" American version begins, "Arise, the workers of all nations! Arise, oppressed of the earth!"

Iron Felix: Felix Dzerzhinsky 1877-1926, was founder of the Cheka, Secret Police, forerunner of the KGB/FSB. His Statue (known throughout Russia as the "Iron Felix") stood in front of the Lubyanka until pulled down in 1991. It was replaced by a (much smaller) memorial plaque for the victims who died in the Gulags. Many former KGB and current FSB men have a small statue of him on their desks to this day.

"Iskateli Priklyucheniy" trans. "Seekers of Adventure".

Kievsky Vokzal: Central Moscow rail/metro station next to the Moscow River. Known to be a very rough and dangerous place after dark.

Kino Palace: Movie House. One depicted here is called Oktyabr and is on Novy Arbat.

Kiosk: Formerly ubiquitous small trailer like structures (street stalls) crowding the Moscow sidewalks. They sell mostly beer, cigarettes, soft drinks and minor grocery items but can basically sell anything with flowers being the most prominent non-food/drink items. Many (but not all) were removed in 2010 in a clean-up campaign by a new Moscow mayor.

Kitai Gorod: Section of Moscow near the Kremlin. Literal translation is China Town and there is still a Chinese presence in this neighborhood. Several popular music and dance clubs can be found here after dark as well. "Kitaiski Letchik Jao Da", trans. "Chinese Pilot Jao Da" is our favorite and the one referenced in the poem Leosha.

Komsomol: Soviet "Young Communist League" . Was open to young people between ages 14 and 28. While membership was not "mandatory" without it University study and advancement within the Soviet System was all but impossible.

Komsomolskaya: Moscow Metro station.

Lada: Used as unregistered gypsy cabs in Moscow and elsewhere. A very small, poorly built, dangerous Soviet era car seldom, if ever, supplied with working seat belts. Less prosperous Russians keep them running for 30 years or more as basic transportation. Still produced in newer, safer models.

Leningradsky Vokzal: Train Station in central Moscow where trains north to St Petersburg and surrounding regions originate from.

Leningradsky Prospekt: A main street that runs out of the center of Moscow starting at

Belorusskaya (where Tverskaya ends) and continuing out of town to Sheremetyevo Airport and beyond eventually becoming the main road to St Petersburg.
Leon: See Trotsky, Leon

Leosha: Alexey Paperny, founder and lead singer of the musical group known as Paperny TAM. Poet, playwright, actor, recording artist, performer. Known by his devoted fans as something akin to a Russian

Bob Dylan. Virtually unknown in the West. His videos can be accessed through You-Tube under Paperny TAM.

Lesnaya Street: Site of our Moscow Apartment Building at 8/12. In central Moscow just off Tverskaya near Belorusskaya. Our neighbor, Anna Politkovskaya, was murdered here.

Lubyanka: Pre Revolutionary building (extensively re-built) in Moscow that housed the original Soviet Security Services which operated under many names (Cheka, NKVD,KGB, etc.) from 1917 through the fall of the Soviet Union. Now HQ of the Border Guards but still housing a prison.

Luzhkov, Yury, Born 1936: Mayor of Moscow 1992-2010. Wife, Yelena Baturina, started as a technician but is now Russia's richest woman with an estimated fortune of over $4 billion USD based on Moscow construction projects.

Makarov: Russian manufactured semi-automatic pistol.

Maximalism: In Marxist theory defined as a "theory of a maximum program of demands that will achieve socialism".

Mayakovski, Vladimir 1893-1930: Very fine Russian Revolutionary Bolshevik Futurist Poet. His statue in front of the Tchaikovsky Concert Hall facing Tverskaya is the assembly point for what remains of the Communist Party of Russia for their May Day march on May 1 every year.

Miramistin: Russian antiseptic (first developed as part of the Soviet Space program to reduce bacteria on Cosmonauts skin and equipment) is widely used in Russia as a prophylactic for STD's.

MVD: Ministry of Internal Affairs/Russian National Police Force/ Politsiya (police) aka under their old name, Militsiya (militia). Totally corrupt, pay as you go. Road Police (also under the MVD) even worse.

"Ne govoryu po-Russki", "Не говорю по-русски": trans. "Sorry, I don't speak Russian."

Night Flight: Famous Moscow restaurant and nightclub open since 1992 on Tverskaya Street near Pushkin Square. Well known to be populated by independent, high end, English speaking working girls. Club caters mostly to non-Russians.

9th of May: Russian National Holiday marking the end of the Great Patriotic War on May 9, 1945.

Novy Arbat: Six lane "new" Arbat Street cut through the old Arbat district in Soviet times destroying many historic structures. Lined with incredibly ugly Soviet Style high rise buildings constructed between 1962 and 1968. Entertainment and shopping district.

OMON: "Otryad Mobilniy Osobogo Nazacheniya" trans. "Special Purpose Mobile Unit". Riot police of the MVD. Also for hire to the highest bidder.

Park Kulturi: Moscow Metro Station.

Petrovka Street: Fine old well preserved Moscow 19th century streetscape running several blocks over and roughly parallel to Tverskaya. Ends right at the Old Bolshoi.

Pioneers: Young Pioneers Organization of the Soviet Union (active 1922-1991) for all children aged 10-15. Combined Boys and Girls organized nationwide activity that included political and moral instruction. Soviet Boy Scouts and Girl Scouts combined. Pioneers wore distinctive red scarves as a badge of honor.

Politkovskaya, Anna 1958-2006: Renowned Russian-American journalist who specialized, in her last years, in exposing Russian Government abuses of human rights in Chechnya. Murdered in the elevator of her apartment building at Lesnaya 8/12 on October 7, 2006, Putin's birthday.

Pol-Pot 1925-1998: General Permanent Party Secretary of the Communist Party then Prime Minister of Kampuchea (Cambodia) from 1963-1979. During the "Khmer Rouge" period of his rule in the late 1970's it is estimated that between 1.7 and 2.2 million Cambodians lost their lives.

Potemkin: Russian Battleship that was subject to a munity by its crew in 1905. Famous pre-revolutionary moment captured by Sergei Eisenstein in his 1925 revolutionary propaganda film, "Battleship Potemkin". Trotsky wrote an introduction for Russian prints of this film.

Producti: A small Russian convenience store in a building (as opposed to a Kiosk on the street) selling Vodka, Beer, Cigarettes and light grocery and household items.

Pushkin, Alexander 1799-1837: Poet of the Russian Romantic period. Revered by many Russians and around the world as the greatest Russian poet of all time.

Pushkin Square: Most famous square in Moscow bisected by Tverskaya Street. Center for demonstrations and other political activity from all parts of the spectrum as well as the site of Russia's first McDonalds which opened in 1990 which was a major national event. Main statue of the poet Pushkin is placed here on the East side of the square.

St. Basil's: Iconic Russian Orthodox Cathedral on Red Square built in 1588 by Ivan the Terrible. Facade is probably the most commonly reproduced image of Russia.

Shashlik: Quintessential Russian dish. Shish kebab mostly of Pork and Lamb but can be Beef, Chicken and even Fish. Best cooked outdoors in Summer by a wood fire.

Sheremetyevo: Original International Airport of Moscow now sharing overseas traffic with Domodedovo. Split ownership between Aeroflot and the Russian Ministry of Transport. Famous in 2013 as home for some weeks to the American NSA "leaker" Edward Snowden.

Siloviki: trans. "People of Force", Politicians who's origins are in the Military and Security Services who came to full power with the rise of Putin.

Slava: Irreplaceable, great Moscow disco with an age and economic level "mixed" Russian crowd (almost no foreigners there) destroyed in the 2007 time frame by an "accidental" fire after a licensing "dispute" with City authorities.

Stalingrad (now Volgograd): Battle of Stalingrad was the major turning point in Russia's favor in the Great Patriotic War. Terrible devastation here.

Smolenskaya: Area of Moscow on the Garden Ring near Stary Arbat. Metro station and exclusive shopping complex bear this name.

Stary Arbat: trans, "Old Arbat". District now dominated by tourist souvenir oriented shops and some good restaurants. First Starbucks in Russia opened here.

Stolovaya: Workers cafeteria in Soviet times with a few remaining original examples in Moscow. The one mentioned here is in the Bus Garage at 20 Lesnaya. "Upscale" version with excellent food though still cafeteria style is in GUM on Red Square and known as Stolovaya 57.

Subbotnik: Bolshevik tradition, voluntary Spring cleaning brigade traditionally organized near Lenin's birthday. First All Russian Subbotnik was held on May 1,1920 and Lenin participated by removing rubble from the Kremlin.

Trotsky, Leon 1879-1940: Hero of the October Revolution, Founder of the Red Army. Anti-Stalin activist expelled from Russia in 1929 who later founded the Fourth International. Assassinated on Stalin's order in Mexico in 1940.

Tverskaya Street: "Main Street" of Moscow. Renamed Gorky Street in Soviet times (1935-1990) and then returned to the original name. Runs north from the foot of the Kremlin to the Garden Ring and then as First Tverskaya Yamskaya to Belorusskaya where it becomes Leningradsky Prospekt.

Veliky Novgorod: World Heritage Site. Ancient town 90 miles south of St Petersburg. Founded in the 9th Century AD.

Vokzal: trans. Train Station.

Volga: Longest river on the European Continent. Major national river of Russia in both historical significance and in commerce.

Volodya: As used here in several poems always refers to Vladimir Putin, Born 1952, KGB Officer 1975-1991, St Petersburg/Moscow Political Adviser and Politician 1991-1998, FSB Director 1998-1999, Acting President of Russia 1999-2000, President of Russia 2000-2008, Prime Minister 2008-2012, President for Life, 2012- ?

Yeltsin, Boris 1931-2007: 1st President of Russia 1991-1999. Soviet "apparatchik" appointed "First Secretary of the Moscow Communist Party" (Mayor of Moscow) in 1985. Rose to full prominence as a "rebel" after being dismissed from his post in 1988. After the failed 1991 Communist Party/KGB coup against Gorbachev he became Russia's 1st President, dissolved the Communist Party and presided over the dissolution of the Soviet Union. His embrace of the disastrous, Washington/CIA sponsored economic policy known as "shock therapy" led to the rise of the "oligarchs", the 1998 financial "crisis" and the subsequent rise of FSB Director Putin who was appointed "temporary" President upon Yeltsin's resignation in 1999. A lifelong alcoholic he surprisingly survived till 2007 and is buried in Novodevichy Cemetery along with such political notables as Khrushchev, Molotov and Gromyko and artistic greats Mayakovski, Chekhov, Eisenstein and Shostakovich.

Yesenin, Sergei 1895-1925: Greatest and most renowned Russian

Lyrical Poet of the 20th Century. Married briefly (1922-23) to the famed American dancer and choreographer Isadora Duncan. Most common portrayal of Yesenin in the West is from the popular 1968 Hollywood film "Isadora". He is very poorly translated and thus nowhere near as well known in the West as he should be though he is still widely revered in Russia and by most literate Russian speakers worldwide.

Zavtra: trans. Tomorrow.

Zolotoy: trans. Gold.

Acknowledgements

The author would first like to acknowledge the people of Moscow and its environs. Without you there would, of course, be no book and I would not have learned a lifetime of lessons, both good and otherwise, in a few short years. What you must live and deal with there can't be fully explained to the uninitiated but I dearly hope that my respect and admiration of your daily struggles comes through in these pages as I attempt to shed some light on what I saw and felt there. I wish you better days.

Two younger Russian men stood out in both personal loyalty and courage in their work with me there and I am forever in their debt.

Aleksey Zherzdev, driver and assistant extraordinaire, saw me through not only the daily horrendous traffic and countless 3:00 AM trips to Sheremetyevo or Domodedovo but became a good friend as well. His quintessentially Russian humor and steadfast devotion to duty will never be forgotten.

Maxim Soldatkin, with his near perfect English, did his best to steer me through the endless frustrations of doing business in Russia while mastering the art himself. It was a privilege and honor to work closely with him as we learned from each other, in equal proportion I think, about the ever-present peril involved in trying to do anything of substance there. I consider Max a friend for life.

The woman to whom this book is dedicated, the incredible Gulbatira (Guli) Abdigalimova, is the finest partner any man could dream of. She is the beginning and the end for me and our years together have deepened and grown both with a sense of wonder and the gratitude which I hope becomes evident to the readers of these poems. That first walk in the snow with her in Moscow is forever with me.

John Huey's student work of the 60's-70's was influenced by teachers in Vermont such as John Irving at Windham College and William Meredith at Bread Loaf.

After many years of involvement in an ongoing international business career that involved travel to over 90 different countries (including an intense, sometimes perilous, engagement with Russia between 2004-2013) he returned to writing poetry in 2011.

Recently he has had poems presented in two issues of *Poetry Quarterly* and in the *Temptation* anthology published in London by Lost Tower Publications. Work has also appeared in *Leannan Magazine, Sein und Werden,* at *In Between Hangovers, Red Wolf Journal, The Lost River Review* and *Perfume River Poetry Review.* A poem regarding the Trump inauguration will appear shortly in an anthology to be published by Poets for Sanctuary (formerly known as Poets Against Trump). *The Moscow Poetry File* is his first full length publication.

His second full length book of poems, *The Far Visible,* was completed in 2016 and is now under review for publication.

In 2017 Huey is in the final stages of a yet to be titled, 70 longer form poem book, involving the years 1966-1972. He was a 'charter member' of that generation and has not been satisfied with much of what he has seen in print and on film about that often trivialized and misunderstood era. This new work is an attempt to take another look at those years and to hopefully contribute to the ongoing study of those times.

In 2018, he is planning to start work in earnest on his first novel, *The Lost Andy's,* and he is looking forward to that adventure.

Further information is available on the web at www.john-huey.com.

www.ingramcontent.com/pod-product-compliance
Lightning Source LLC
Chambersburg PA
CBHW021146090426
42740CB00008B/960